"I tell my students, 'If you find yourself in the company of people who agree with you, you're in the wrong company.'"

—Condoleezza Rice

CONDOLEEZZA RICE: U.S. SECRETARY OF STATE

BY KEVIN CUNNINGHAM

Content Adviser: Antonia Felix,
Condoleezza Rice biographer

Published in the United States of America by The Child's World®
PO Box 326
Chanhassen, MN 55317-0326
800-599-READ
www.childsworld.com

The Child's World®: Mary Berendes, Publishing Director
Editorial Directions, Inc.: E. Russell Primm, Editorial Director; Emily J. Dolbear,
Line Editor; Katie Marsico, Assistant Editor; Matthew Messbarger, Editorial Assistant;
Susan Hindman, Copy Editor; Sarah E. De Capua, Proofreader; Marsha Bonnoit,
Peter Garnham, Terry Johnson, Chris Simms, and Stephan Carl Wender,
Fact Checkers; Tim Griffin/IndexServ, Indexer; Dawn Friedman,
Photo Researcher; Linda S. Koutris, Photo Selector

The Child's World® and Journey to Freedom® are the sole property
and registered trademarks of The Child's World®

Cover photograph: Condoleezza Rice in 2003 / © Reuters NewMedia, Inc./Corbis

Interior photographs © AP/Wide World Photos: 11, 14; Barry Thumma/AP/Wide World Photos: 24;
Lionel Cironneau/AP/Wide World Photos: 26; J. Scott Applewhite/AP/Wide World Photos: 31; Jim
Collins/AP/Wide World Photos: 32; Center for a New Generation, a program of the Boys and Girls Club
of the Peninsula: 28; Reuters NewMedia, Inc./Corbis: 2, 36; Bettmann/Corbis: 16, 17; Morton Beebe,
S.F./Corbis: 19; AFP/Corbis: 22, 33; Peter Turnley/Corbis: 25, 27; New York Times Co./Getty Images: 9;
Tome Hauck/Getty Images: 15; Alex Wong/Getty Images: 35; Chuck Painter/Stanford University
News Service: 21; Linda A. Cicero/Stanford University News Service: 29; Stillman College
Archives: 12; University of Denver Special Collections and Archives: 6, 10, 13, 18.

Library of Congress Cataloging-in-Publication Data
Cunningham, Kevin, 1966–
Condoleezza Rice : U.S. Secretary of State / by Kevin Cunningham.
v. cm. — (Journey to freedom)
Includes bibliographical references and index.
Contents: Daughter of teachers — A change of plans — A booming career — Today and tomorrow —
Timeline.
ISBN 1-59296-231-9 (library bound : alk. paper) 1. Rice, Condoleezza, 1954– —Juvenile literature. 2. National
Security Council (U.S.)—Biography—Juvenile literature. 3. African American women educators—
Biography—Juvenile literature. 4. International relations specialists—United States—Biography—Juvenile lit-
erature. [1. Rice, Condoleezza, 1954- 2. National Security Council (U.S.)—Biography. 3. Women—Biography.
4. African Americans—Biography.] I. Title. II. Series.
UA23.15.C85 2004
355'.033073'092—dc21   2003027077

Contents

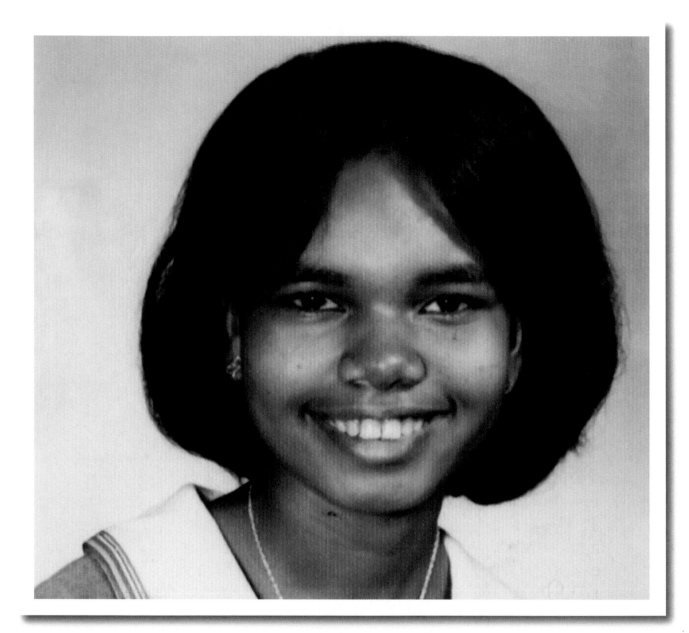

CONDOLEEZZA RICE WAS THE ONLY CHILD OF TWO TEACHERS. THE RICES RAISED THEIR DAUGHTER TO VALUE EDUCATION.

Daughter of Teachers

On November 14, 1954, Condoleezza Rice was born in Birmingham, Alabama. Both her parents had college educations, which was unusual for African-Americans in Birmingham at the time. John Wesley Rice, an educator and a Presbyterian minister, had married Angelena Ray, a teacher who played the piano and organ, in the early 1950s. Angelena named their daughter for the Italian musical term *con dolcezza,* which instructs a performer to play "with sweetness."

From the start, the Rices were determined to educate their daughter. Before beginning school, many children learn the alphabet, their colors, and maybe some reading. Condoleezza could read, play piano, and had studied French, ballet, and art before kindergarten. When she did start school, she was so far ahead that she skipped the first grade and later the seventh grade. "I had parents who gave me every conceivable opportunity," Condoleezza Rice said years later. "They also believed in achievement."

Angelena Rice took music seriously. Condoleezza's mother, grandmother, and great-grandmother all played piano. Her grandmother was also a piano teacher. Condoleezza (or Condi) liked to watch and listen to her grandmother's students. Often she would pound on the keys, trying to play. At age three, she began taking lessons from her grandmother. Condoleezza could read sheet music before she could even read books.

From an early age, she showed a striking desire to learn. "Condoleezza's always been so focused, ever since she was really, really young," one of her aunts has said. "She would practice her piano at a certain time without anyone having to remind her." By the time she was four, she had learned enough piano pieces to give her first performance.

Because Condoleezza could already read at age five, Angelena tried to put her in school. But the principal said she was too young. So Angelena took a year off from work to teach her daughter at home. In addition to schoolwork, Condoleezza continued piano lessons. Her mother also took her to museums to learn about art.

At the time, Alabama and all of the southern states were **segregated.** For years, whites had passed laws to separate themselves from African-Americans in almost every place possible, including public bath-rooms, movie theaters, and schools. These laws, called Jim Crow laws, were meant to separate the races. The laws also humiliated African-Americans. For example, it was against the law for an African-American even to offer to shake a white man's hand.

The Rices prepared Condoleezza for the reality of the Jim Crow laws in three ways. First, they protected their daughter. When she heard ugly comments or saw Jim Crow laws in action, Condoleezza was told, "It's not your problem." Second, the Rices refused to play along. If they encountered **racism,** they demanded calmly and firmly to be treated as equals to whites. Third, they made sure Condoleezza would succeed in the white society that valued education. Birmingham's educated black community knew their children would have to be twice as smart and twice as talented as whites to get respect. Condoleezza worked to be both.

As a child, Condoleezza Rice lived in a segregated society. Laws in the South called Jim Crow laws required black customers at this theater to go to a separate entrance.

It wasn't all work. Every Sunday, she and her father would sit on the couch watching football games on television. But it wasn't idle viewing. John Rice, a former school coach who had hoped for a son to talk football with, decided to teach the game to his daughter instead. In typical Rice fashion, Condoleezza's father explained the plays, the teams, and the rules to her. She developed a lifelong love of the game.

As Condoleezza grew older, she became aware of trouble around her. Through the 1950s, the **civil rights movement** began to oppose racist laws and demand that those laws be thrown out. African-Americans and some whites banded together to fight for **integrated** schools, the right of all blacks to vote, and other political and social changes.

HERE CONDOLEEZZA'S FATHER, JOHN WESLEY RICE, SPEAKS AT THE UNIVERSITY OF DENVER, WHERE HE TAUGHT ABOUT THE AFRICAN-AMERICAN EXPERIENCE IN A COURSE CALLED BLACK STUDIES IN THE 1970s.

By the early 1960s, the movement began to succeed. Whites in the southern states fought back with threats and violence. So many bombs went off in Birmingham that the city was nicknamed Bombingham. Bomb threats forced Condoleezza to miss many days of school. On September 15, 1963, a tragedy touched Condoleezza personally. During Sunday school at the Sixteenth Street Baptist Church, a bomb exploded, killing four girls. One of those girls was Denise McNair, a friend of Condoleezza's.

The civil rights movement marched ahead despite the violence. In 1964, President Lyndon Johnson signed the Civil Rights Act, ending legal segregation. A few days later, the Rices entered—and were served at— a formerly whites-only restaurant.

THE BOMB THAT EXPLODED AT THE SIXTEENTH STREET BAPTIST CHURCH ON SEPTEMBER 15, 1963, PRODUCED THIS LARGE CRATER. FOUR BLACK GIRLS WERE KILLED, INCLUDING A FRIEND OF CONDOLEEZZA'S.

The next year, Condoleezza's father took a job as dean of students at Stillman College in Tuscaloosa, Alabama. In 1969, John Rice earned his **master's degree,** got a job at the University of Denver, and moved his family to Colorado.

Condoleezza enrolled at St. Mary's Academy. It was the first integrated school she had ever attended. The students were smart and driven, like her. Condoleezza's mature behavior and self-confidence—as well as her intellect—amazed teachers.

In Condoleezza's senior year of high school, she already had enough credits to graduate. Her parents wanted her to start college. But in a rare moment of rebellion, she asked to finish high school with her friends. The Rices agreed, but only if Condoleezza started college part-time. So in addition to her high school classes, piano lessons, and ice-skating, she took college courses at the University of Denver.

After winning a piano contest, Condoleezza played with the Denver Symphony Orchestra. A career in music awaited her. Then she surprised everyone, including herself, by turning onto a new path—one that would lead to the White House.

CONDOLEEZZA ATTENDS AN EVENT AT STILLMAN COLLEGE WITH HER PARENTS IN 1967.

A Change of Plans

Condoleezza Rice entered the university full-time at the age of 16. She studied piano until her second year in college. The following summer, she performed at a music festival in nearby Aspen, Colorado. There she competed against 11-year-olds more advanced than she was. While an excellent musician, Rice knew only the most brilliant became concert pianists. She did not want to teach or direct a church choir. If she was only "pretty good but not great," as she said, she preferred to switch to a field where she could be great.

It was a hard decision. Her parents had spent a lot of time and money training her for piano. Now she wanted to study something else. She didn't even know *what* to study. She tried government, but the classes bored her. She tried English literature, but she hated it.

AT THE UNIVERSITY OF DENVER, RICE DECIDED AGAINST A MUSIC CAREER.

One day in the spring of her third year of college, Rice heard a speech about Joseph Stalin, the **dictator** of the Soviet Union. The Soviet Union was the large Eastern European country—of which Russia was a part—that followed a form of government called **Communism** from 1922 to 1991. The man giving the speech, Dr. Josef Korbel, fascinated her. "I remember thinking, Russia is a place I want to know more about," she later said.

Impressed with her intelligence, Korbel suggested Rice consider **international relations.** Korbel became her **mentor.** On his advice, she began to study Russian history and the Russian language. After that, she studied "Soviet politics, Soviet everything."

Though she came late to her new field of study, Rice studied hard and graduated with honors in 1974. She won an award for "outstanding accomplishment and promise in the field of political science." The school also named her Outstanding Senior Woman.

Anyone going into a career in international relations needs more than one college degree. Condoleezza Rice headed east to the University of Notre Dame in Indiana to earn her master's degree. The school was famous for combining a religious education with its academic classes. Rice, a very religious person from a religious family, liked that. So did her father.

Rice had witnessed the civil rights movement. Now she studied an even bigger conflict called the **Cold War.**

After World War II (1939–1945), much of the world separated into two groups: nations that followed Communism and nations that believed in democracy. In democratic countries like the United States and Great Britain, the people voted for their leaders. These countries followed capitalism, a system in which individuals and companies decide what to make and buy. In Communist countries such as the Soviet Union, the government owned everything. These countries controlled the outcome of elections as well as many other aspects of daily life. The Soviet government forced many other countries in Eastern Europe to become Communist.

Condoleezza Rice became interested in the Cold War and in how the Soviet Union used its power. Her study of the Soviet military—its army, navy, and air force—would become a major part of her life.

THE SOVIET UNION AND ITS MILITARY POWER FASCINATED RICE. IN THIS 1977 PHOTOGRAPH, TANKS ROLL THROUGH MOSCOW'S RED SQUARE DURING A MILITARY PARADE CELEBRATING THE SOVIET UNION'S 60TH ANNIVERSARY.

Rice did well at Notre Dame. Her teachers had to create a special program for her because the regular classes weren't challenging enough. As the year ended, Rice thought about going to law school. Korbel did not agree. "You are very talented," he said. "You have to become a professor." She had never considered that possibility. In August 1975, 20-year-old Condoleezza Rice graduated with her master's degree. Soon she returned to the University of Denver and began work on her **PhD.**

A doctorate normally takes years to earn. As usual, Rice threw herself into her studies. She worked as an intern with the U.S. Department of State in Washington, D.C., in 1977. Her research gave her a chance to go to the Soviet Union and see up close what she had read so much about at school. It wasn't easy, though. The Soviets kept almost everything a secret.

JOSEF KORBEL URGED RICE TO CONTINUE HER STUDIES. HIS DAUGHTER, MADELEINE ALBRIGHT, BECAME THE COUNTRY'S FIRST WOMAN SECRETARY OF STATE IN 1997.

Rice also became engaged. To no one's surprise, the huge football fan fell in love with a member of the Denver Broncos. It was so serious she began to sit with other players' wives at games. The relationship ended, however. As with most things about her personal life, she has kept the details private.

On August 14, 1981, Condoleezza Rice graduated with her PhD. Friends and family members came to the ceremonies. Unfortunately, Korbel was not there to see it. He died of stomach cancer in 1977. By graduation day, Rice already had a job lined up at Stanford University in Palo Alto, California.

A Booming Career

As an expert in international relations, Condoleezza Rice was special in many ways. First, of course, she was intelligent. Some of her professors had a harder time learning Russian than she did. Second, as most political scientists were white men, being an African-American woman in the field made Rice truly rare. She was well aware of this fact.

Rice enjoyed her teaching job at Stanford. Her energy, outgoing personality, and ability to back up strong opinions made her an ideal teacher. So did her race and sex. The university told Rice, however, that when it was time to award permanent jobs, an African-American woman would get no special treatment.

Not that she needed any. Rice immediately became one of Stanford's most popular professors. In 1984, the university gave her its highest award for teaching. Over the next few years, she was promoted to full professor, the top of the ladder for teachers. In that time, she won another award for teaching and wrote three books.

Unfortunately, all of this work kept her away from her parents, who still lived in Denver. Angelena Rice became sicker and sicker from breast cancer and died in 1985 at age 61. After the funeral service, Rice played some of her mother's favorite hymns on the piano as a tribute to her love of music.

CONDOLEEZZA RICE WAS A POPULAR AND ENERGETIC TEACHER AT STANFORD UNIVERSITY.

In addition to her academic responsibilities, Rice worked for the Council on Foreign Relations in Washington, D.C. This group studied and reported on America's relationships with other countries, especially Communist nations. Rice saw how the U.S. military worked, made decisions, and planned ahead. That experience would prove to be valuable.

In Palo Alto, Rice built a life outside work. After arriving at Stanford, she played organ for six months at a nearby church. She continued to follow football—sometimes watching 12 hours a day. She joked that she could write more books if there was less football on television.

Like her father, Rice was interested in serving the community. John Rice had headed a Boy Scout troop, taught, coached, and done church work. In 1986, Condoleezza joined a group that helped train minority students for work and college. At Stanford, too, Rice served on many committees.

Meanwhile, the outside world was changing faster than anyone had predicted. By the late 1980s, citizens in Eastern Europe were demanding reform, and the Soviet Union was ready to collapse. If it fell apart, the Cold War might finally end. No one knew what would happen. It was a confusing and dangerous time.

CONDOLEEZZA RICE HAS ALWAYS MAINTAINED A BUSY SCHEDULE. SHE BALANCES MANY ACTIVITIES, INCLUDING COMMUNITY WORK, PIANO PLAYING, AND EXERCISE.

PRESIDENT GEORGE H. W. BUSH WALKS WITH HIS NATIONAL
SECURITY ADVISER, BRENT SCOWCROFT, WHO HIRED RICE TO
ADVISE HIM IN 1989.

George H. W. Bush, the new president, needed experts on the Soviet Union. He had chosen a man named Brent Scowcroft to be national security adviser—the position Rice would hold 12 years later. Scowcroft had met Rice at Stanford. "Here was this slip of a girl," he said later. "Boy, she held her own. I said, 'That's someone I've got to get to know.'" Now he needed her in Washington to practice what she had preached for so long as a teacher.

In 1989, Rice took over as director of Soviet and Eastern European affairs on the National Security Council. One of her first major assignments was to report on Soviet leader Mikhail Gorbachev. Having studied Gorbachev for years, Rice laid out a four-part plan for dealing with him and the Soviet Union.

MIKHAIL GORBACHEV WAS LEADER OF THE SOVIET UNION WHEN RICE STARTED WORKING FOR THE NATIONAL SECURITY COUNCIL IN 1989.

Finally, the Berlin Wall came down in 1989. Since its construction in 1961, the Berlin Wall had prevented the East Germans, who lived under Communism, from escaping to democratic West Germany. To everyone's amazement, the government of East Germany did not fight against it. Gorbachev asked for a meeting with U.S. officials to discuss letting East Germany and West Germany become one nation again.

Rice sat at the table with Bush and Gorbachev. When the two men met, Bush said, "This is Condoleezza Rice. She tells me everything I know about the Soviet Union." The Soviets, used to dealing with older white men, didn't know what to think of her.

ON NOVEMBER 12, 1989, MANY EAST GERMANS FLOODED THROUGH THE DISMANTLED BERLIN WALL INTO WEST BERLIN. THE FALL OF THE HISTORIC BERLIN WALL CHANGED U.S.-SOVIET RELATIONS FOREVER.

Behind the scenes, Rice insisted the two Germanys become one as soon as possible. Otherwise, the Soviets might interfere. Many people thought it was a risky move. Rice turned out to be right. In less than a year, Germany reunited. Less than a year after that, Russians voted for their own president. On Christmas Day 1991, Gorbachev stepped down, and the Soviet Union soon came to an end.

With all of these changes in motion, Rice decided to return to Stanford University. Working for the government left little time for a personal life. She thought about starting a family. Teaching and advising students meant a lot to her. There were books to write and people to meet. So she left Washington to share her experiences with her students.

She also resumed her life outside of work. Inspired by a trip to a local middle school, Rice teamed with her father and his second wife to start the Center for a New Generation. It is an after-school program in which promising students are trained in language and performing arts, computers, math, and science. Stanford students do the teaching. "Those are sort of my kids," she said of the children in the program. "All 125 of them."

COLIN POWELL, THE COUN-TRY'S FIRST BLACK NATIONAL SECURITY ADVISER, CAME TO A CENTER FOR A NEW GEN-ERATION EVENT IN 1998.

Condoleezza Rice also took a new job at Stanford. In 1993, she became provost of the university. As provost, she managed the university's $1.5 billion budget and made decisions that affected the entire school. Not only was she the first woman and African-American to hold the job, at the age of 38, she was also the youngest. The same year, Stanford made her a full professor. Soon, *Time* magazine declared her one of "50 Young Leaders to Watch." That prediction proved to be true.

CONDOLEEZZA RICE WAS APPOINTED PROVOST OF STANFORD UNIVERSITY IN 1993.

Today and Tomorrow

Rice had become close friends with the Bush family. She helped the former president and Scowcroft write a book about the end of Communism and the Persian Gulf War of 1991. So when George W. Bush, the president's son, decided to run for president, Rice agreed to advise him on world affairs.

Rice and Bush were friends from the start. George W., a big baseball fan (he was once an owner of the Texas Rangers), enjoyed listening to Rice's stories about the legendary player Willie Mays, who was one of her mother's students in Birmingham. "Governor Bush was very impressed," she later said.

Bush also was impressed with Rice's knowledge. Dealing with other countries is a big part of being president, and Bush had to be able to answer questions on many different world problems. Since he didn't like studying alone, he asked Rice and another adviser to prepare him by answering his questions in detail. Sometimes they talked while exercising or fishing.

When George W. Bush won the presidential election in 2000, he did not hesitate to appoint his adviser and close friend to the important job of national security adviser. Condoleezza Rice became the first woman to hold the position. Sadly, just six days later, her father died.

During her earlier time in government, Condoleezza Rice had witnessed up close many changes in the world. As she settled into her new job, she had no idea of the dramatic changes that were about to take place in the world.

GEORGE W. BUSH LISTENS TO CONDOLEEZZA RICE AFTER NAMING HER
NATIONAL SECURITY ADVISER DURING A 2000 CEREMONY IN AUSTIN, TEXAS.
RICE WAS THE FIRST WOMAN EVER APPOINTED TO THE POSITION.

On the morning of September 11, 2001, terrorists hijacked four planes. Two hit the towers of the World Trade Center in New York City. A third plowed into the Pentagon, the headquarters of the U.S. Department of Defense near Washington, D.C. The fourth plane, believed to have been on its way to the White House or the U.S. Capitol in Washington, crashed in Pennsylvania. Rice immediately called her aunt and uncle in Birmingham, told them she was safe, and got to work.

Soon an investigation pegged the hijackers as members of al-Qaeda, a terrorist organization led by Saudi Arabian millionaire Osama bin Laden. Plans had to be made about how to respond.

THE SOUTH TOWER COLLAPSES AS SMOKE BILLOWS FROM THE TWIN 110-STORY TOWERS OF THE WORLD TRADE CENTER ON SEPTEMBER 11, 2001.

When the president decided to attack al-Qaeda in its main hiding place—Afghanistan—Rice was part of the team that created the so-called Bush Doctrine. This policy declared the United States would defeat terrorist organizations like al-Qaeda. It would also attack countries that hid or helped these organizations.

During the military campaign in Afghanistan, Rice spent a lot of time with President Bush. She went with him on trips to Camp David (the presidential retreat) and to his ranch in Texas. Rice now had to keep informed about many countries in addition to Russia. She was responsible for all kinds of details. For example, Rice helped come up with the idea to drop food packages inside Afghanistan for civilians.

CONDOLEEZZA RICE IS A TRUSTED ADVISER OF GEORGE W. BUSH. THE PRESIDENT AND RICE CONFER ON THE SOUTH LAWN OF THE WHITE HOUSE BEFORE FLYING TO NEARBY CAMP DAVID IN 2002.

The United States defeated Afghanistan's government in five weeks. President Bush and his advisers turned their attention to another country they believed helped terrorists—Iraq. For a time, various people in government disagreed about what to do. Some wanted war. Others preferred to work with the United Nations to apply pressure on Iraq.

Rice believed Iraq's dictator, Saddam Hussein, was dangerous. When President Bush decided to go to war, Rice explained why the United States needed to attack and what it needed to do. One of the main dangers, she said, was that Hussein might have chemical, biological, or nuclear weapons.

Some people asked for a "smoking gun," meaning evidence that Hussein had such weapons. "We don't want the smoking gun to be a mushroom cloud," Rice said, referring to the cloud that appears after a nuclear bomb explosion. In her view, Iraq could soon build nuclear bombs and had used chemical weapons before. The country also trained terrorists. All those things, she claimed, made it necessary to go to war.

Rice made her feelings very clear in August 2003, after Hussein had been defeated. "Saddam Hussein's regime posed a threat to the security of the United States and the world. . . . That threat could not be allowed to remain," Rice said.

As the Iraq war continued, however, Rice faced criticism about the lack of weapons of mass destruction (WMDs) in Iraq. She did not back down and responded to the criticism by stating that the Iraq invasion was still needed as a means to stop Saddam Hussein from developing WMDs.

In April 2004, Rice agreed to appear before the commission investigating the September 11 terrorist attacks. During her testimony, she said everything possible had been done to prevent terrorism in America. Her statements and answers to the commission's questions began one of the biggest controversies of her career.

During the presidential campaign, Rice broke with tradition and made speeches across the country on behalf of President Bush. Shortly after his re-election, she told him she wished to serve during his second term. He asked her to replace Colin Powell as secretary of state, the country's top diplomat. Many considered it an ideal fit because Rice and the president had a close working relationship. According to aides, they know each other so well that they communicate via body language as much as through words.

On November 16, 2004, President Bush nominated Rice for secretary of state saying, "Above all, Dr. Rice has a deep, abiding belief in the value and power of liberty, because she has seen freedom denied and freedom reborn."

Condoleezza Rice has always moved from one challenge to another. Undoubtedly, she isn't through yet. Some think she would make an excellent governor or university president. Others wonder if she will run for president of the United States. She leaves no doubt about her dream job, though—running the National Football League. "Anybody who really

RICE IS A FREQUENT GUEST ON THE COUNTRY'S TELEVISION NEWS PROGRAMS. ON THIS 2003 VISIT TO *MEET THE PRESS*, SHE DISCUSSED THE SITUATION IN IRAQ.

knows me knows that that's absolutely true," she once said, "and that if the NFL job comes up, [President Bush] is on his own."

I'm glad she's put those plans on hold once again," President Bush said after nominating her for secretary of state. "The nation needs her."

Condoleezza Rice's strength of mind, determination, and talent have made this daughter of teachers from Birmingham the best-known African-American woman in the world. It's hard to believe anything can stop her. "I'm a really religious person," she says, "and I don't believe that I was put on this earth to be sour, so I'm eternally optimistic about things."

CONDOLEEZZA RICE GIVES A THUMBS-UP AS SHE WAITS FOR THE PRESIDENT TO LAND ON THE AIRCRAFT CARRIER USS *ABRAHAM LINCOLN*, ON MAY 1, 2003. FROM THE CARRIER'S DECK, BUSH ANNOUNCED TO THE NATION THAT ALL MAJOR COMBAT IN IRAQ HAD ENDED.

Timeline

1954	On November 14, Condoleezza Rice is born to John Wesley and Angelena Ray Rice in Birmingham, Alabama.
1963	On September 15, a bomb set by the Ku Klux Klan explodes at Birmingham's Sixteenth Street Baptist Church. Four girls, including an 11-year-old friend of Condoleezza's, Denise McNair, die in the blast.
1965	Rice enters the Birmingham Southern Conservatory of Music to study piano, flute, and violin. John Rice becomes dean of students at Stillman College. The Rices move to Tuscaloosa, Alabama.
1969	John Rice gets a job at the University of Denver. The Rice family moves to Denver, where Condoleezza attends an integrated school for the first time.
1974	Rice graduates with honors from the University of Denver at the age of 19.
1975	Rice earns her master's degree in government from the University of Notre Dame.
1977	Rice works as an intern with the U.S. Department of State.
1981	Rice earns her PhD from the Graduate School of International Studies at the University of Denver.
1984	Rice wins Stanford University's highest award for teaching. That same year, she publishes her first book, *Uncertain Allegiance: The Soviet Union and the Czechoslovak Army*.
1986	Rice publishes (with Alexander Dallin) her second book, *The Gorbachev Era*.
1987	Rice becomes an associate professor of political science at Stanford University.
1989	Rice takes over as director of Soviet and Eastern European Affairs on the National Security Council. Later she is promoted to senior director. She advises President George H. W. Bush on the collapse of the Soviet Union.
1990	Rice sits at the bargaining table during the meetings between U.S. president George H. W. Bush and Soviet leader Mikhail Gorbachev. Later, she serves as presidential adviser during Gorbachev's visit to Washington, D.C.
1991	Rice returns to Stanford as an associate professor.
1993	Rice becomes a full professor and accepts the position of provost at Stanford University. She is the first African-American and the first woman to hold the job. She serves until 1999.
1995	Rice (with Phillip Zelikow) publishes the book *Germany Unified and Europe Transformed*.
1999	Rice advises Texas governor and Republican presidential candidate George W. Bush on foreign policy.
2000	On December 18, Rice is named national security adviser. Six days later, her father dies.
2001	Rice is sworn in as national security adviser.
2002	Rice receives the NAACP (National Association for the Advancement of Colored People) President's Award for leadership in promoting the advancement of minorities. Rice makes her "mushroom cloud" statement about Iraq on September 8.
2003	Rice receives an honorary degree from the Mississippi College School of Law.
2004	President George W. Bush nominates Rice for secretary of state.

Glossary

**civil rights movement
(SIV-il rites MOOV-muhnt)**
The civil rights movement was a series of events that took place in the 1950s and 1960s in the United States. African-Americans and whites joined together to gain equal laws and equal rights for African-Americans. Rice witnessed the civil rights movement.

Cold War (KOLD WOHR)
The Cold War refers to the struggle for world power that took place between the Soviet Union and the United States after World War II ended in 1945. The Cold War ended in 1991, when the Soviet Union collapsed. Because the two sides never fought directly, the conflict was considered "cold," unlike a real "hot" war.

Communism (KOM-yuh-NIZ-uhm)
Communism is a system in which the government owns everything and is supposed to distribute the profits. Under Communism, governments often banned free speech, controlled elections, and used force. Condoleezza Rice learned about Communism during her studies of the Soviet Union.

dictator (DIK-tay-tur)
A dictator is a leader who rules a country unjustly. Joseph Stalin was dictator of the Soviet Union from 1929 to 1953.

integrated (IN-tuh-GRAY-tid)
Integrated means made open to people of all races. In the 1950s and 1960s, the civil rights movement fought for integrated public schools.

**international relations
(IN-ter-NASH-uh-nul ri-LAY-shuhns)**
International relations are the official contacts among governments around the world. Rice is an expert in the field of international relations.

master's degree (MAS-turz duh-GREE)
A master's degree is the degree given to university students after a bachelor's degree (received after completing four years of college) and before a PhD (or doctorate). Most require one or two years of study.

mentor (MEN-tore)
A mentor is a knowledgeable and trusted adviser. Dr. Josef Korbel was Rice's mentor.

PhD (PEE-aych-dee)
PhD is an abbreviation that means "doctorate of philosophy." It is the most advanced degree for university students.

racism (RAY-sih-zim)
Racism is a negative opinion about people because of their race. When the Rice family encountered racism, they demanded to be treated as equals to whites.

segregated (SE-greh-GAY-tid)
Segregated means organized to keep whites and blacks apart by maintaining separate public facilities. When Condoleezza Rice was a child in Alabama, segregated schools and other public facilities were common.

Index

Further Information

Books

Ditchfield, Christin. *Condoleezza Rice: National Security Advisor.* Danbury, Conn.: Franklin Watts, 2003.

Ryan, Bernard. *Condoleezza Rice: National Security Advisor and Musician.* New York: Facts On File, 2003.

Wade, Linda R. *Condoleezza Rice: National Security Advisor.* Hockessin, Del.: Mitchell Lane Publishers, Inc., 2002.

Wade, Mary Dodson. *Condoleezza Rice: Being the Best.* Brookfield, Conn.: Millbrook, 2003.

Web Sites

Visit our homepage for lots of links about Condoleezza Rice:

http://www.childsworld.com/links.html

Note to Parents, Teachers, and Librarians:
We routinely verify our Web links to make sure they're safe, active sites—so encourage your readers to check them out!

About the Author

Kevin Cunningham is an author and travel writer. He studied journalism and history at the University of Illinois at Urbana. As a student, he became interested in African-American culture through studies of the civil rights movement, Harlem Renaissance, and black music. His other books include *The Canadian Americans* and *Arthur Ashe: Athlete and Activist.* He lives in Chicago.